The dangers of the Cornish coast are not only the obviou~ these are the worst. Most winters bring several gales wit.. ..... ~. . ~ ...... ~. ..~~. ~. more and fog can occur at any season.

But the tides too can wreak havoc with an un-wary seaman. In the days of sail a ship could be moved many miles even on a calm day simply by the tide and end up a long way from her expected position.

Until the 18th century charts were very rudimentary affairs and tidal observations virtually unknown. There were no Admiralty Sailing Directions or published Passage Information to list all the hidden rocks and other dangers as we have today. Now we know about the 'circular' tide between Lands End and the Scilly Isles but it must have been a nightmare to any stranger navigating the area in the early days. The tide is called circular or rotatory because it changes direction every two or three hours. Now it is only necessary to know the time of high water at Devonport and to consult a chart to calculate the set of the tide at any time.

The tidal stream is greatly influenced by the coast-line itself. Any prominent headland will deflect its direction and thus affect a ship's course. If a sailing ship was also encountering a strong wind she could easily find herself in trouble on a lee shore. Worse still was to be embayed between two headlands and unable to claw her way out of trouble. Then her only recourse might be to anchor and wait for a shift of wind always supposing the sea-bed provided a good enough holding ground for it. In addition the magnificent promontories like Lands End and the Lizard all have their hidden dangers of submerged rocks lying off-shore with their attendant tide-rips and overfalls to catch the careless navigator.

The entrance to the English Channel has been known for centuries as the 'Chops of the Channel' because of its fancied resemblance on a chart to a gaping mouth. The Cornish coast which forms the upper jaw of this fantasy is certainly armed with many teeth to catch the unlucky sailor.

The Isles of Scilly, although not Cornish territory, surely add a remarkable collection of hazards to this part of the world. The islands number forty-eight all told with countless submerged rocks around them. The tidal streams running between them are very complex although fortunately not very strong. They will produce overfalls at times over the sunken rocks and when combined with the prevailing Atlantic swell can prove hazardous indeed.

Between these islands and Lands End lie the Seven Stones rocks, a most dangerous reef. They cover an area of about two square miles and lie almost 15 miles WNW of Lands End. They only begin to show above water at half-ebb but the sea is constantly breaking on them. In very bad weather the breakers can clearly be seen from the Isles of Scilly seven miles away. The great plume of spray looks remarkably like a steam engine at full speed. This reef is marked by the Seven Stones lightvessel on the Eastern side and her log book records a sombre list of ships wrecked on it. Fortunately survivors from a number of them reached the lightvessel, either by their own boat or rescued by one launched from the lightvessel herself. These were all in the days before radio could summon help quickly.

Wolf Rock Lighthouse. AUTHOR'S COLLECTION

Although Cornwall's lighthouse heritage is only about 600 years old lighthouses have been used by man elsewhere for well over 2,000 years. The earliest recorded ones were included in the classical Seven Wonders of the World. The Colossus at Rhodes was built in 300 BC and was a statue of Apollo 100 feet high holding aloft a flaming torch. It stood for 80 years before an earthquake destroyed it. The Pharos at Alexandria was built in 261 BC and stood until the middle of the 13th century. A truly remarkable building having a height of 450 feet. It was the tallest roofed structure ever built in the whole world until the coming of the American sky-scrapers. It clearly demonstrates that there must have been earlier lights that did not survive, nor were they recorded.

The earliest known British lighthouse was built by the Romans in the first century at Dover. It still survives today and is in the grounds of Dover castle overlooking the harbour.

For centuries after the departure of the Romans little is known of any coast lighting except for local traditions crediting church authorities with the display of certain lights. The clues to this activity are often no more than a Saint's name given to a prominent headland or island e.g. St Mary's Isle near Tynemouth, St Catherine's Point Isle of Wight, St Ann's Head, South Wales and many others. But by Medieval times it was established practice for the Ecclesiastical authorities, Monasteries, Abbeys or Priories to provide lights on the coast. Sometimes funding them by the sale of Indulgences, they often provided the man-power to serve them as well as paying for the fuel. These lights were simple affairs, mainly a fire held in a firebasket or cresset. Occasionally they were candles in a lanthorn usually associated with a port entrance where a lighted fire with flying sparks would be too much of a risk to ship's ropes and canvas sails.

Evidence does exist regarding some of these Ecclesiastical lights in Cornwall. The County Record Office at Truro holds a manuscript recording the grant of the chapel of Cam Brae [sic] to Ralph de Bolauhel in 1396. The previous hermit had died and the grant records that the hermitage was to 'enjoy the money called byckenage [beaconage] receivable from the fishermen . . .'. This seems to imply that a light from the chapel on Cam Brea was exhibited for their use.

Cyril Noall, in his book Cornish Lights and Shipwrecks records another such lighted beacon at St Ives and a written record of it by John Leland in 1538 still exists. This was a light shown from the chapel of St Nicholas on the headland to the north of the town. A fairly modern replacement stands on the spot today but no guiding light is shown since there are more efficient ones at the harbour entrance. Also to be found at St Ives is the old harbour lantern. This is in the museum and was in use prior to 1831 on the West Pier, carrying three candles.

St Michael's Mount in Mount's Bay still has the remnants of a stone lantern which is said to date from the 15th century. It is on the top of the church at the SW corner and the light guided ships into the important harbour there. Douglas Hague records a 14th century light shown from the chapel of St Michael on Rame Head at the entrance to Plymouth Sound. Plymouth municipal records of 1488 show that a watchman was paid to keep and light a beacon here.

Many of these Ecclesiastical lights were lost when Henry VIII dissolved the monasteries as the funds for maintaining and manning them came to an end and their records were lost as well. However history shows that Henry made amends,

Penzance harbour about 1870 with square ended stone barges in foreground. AUTHOR'S COLLECTION

unintentionally perhaps, by bringing into existence the Corporation of Trinity House in 1514 under the guidance of a Master, Wardens and a board of Elder Brethren. In the beginning it was charged with safeguarding the Kingdom simply by providing a supply of efficient pilots. It was much later in its history that its duties comprised the erection and supervision of lighthouses, the role for which it is now justly famous.

Trinity House is now responsible for all the major lighthouses on the coast of Cornwall and the Isles of Scilly. The smaller lights marking the entrance to harbours and rivers are maintained by local lighthouse and harbour authorities throughout the area but all are within the jurisdiction of Trinity House who inspect them at regular intervals.

The major lights are classified by Trinity House as either 'rock' or 'land' stations. After 1975 rock stations were manned by six men instead of four and they served four weeks on and four weeks off duty, three men at a time. This has been changed by the coming of automation and all Cornish rock stations are un-manned and fully automated.

Prior to 1975 the keepers served eight weeks on duty and four weeks off, with only four men to a station. All reliefs were carried out by ship or local boatmen. They received extra pay, known as Rock Allowance, to compensate for hardship at such isolated places.

After October 1992 conditions at land stations also improved. The complement at these stations was been increased from four to six with each man serving four weeks on and four off. Those who were living at each station in 1992 still used the lighthouse dwellings and the others lived in their own homes off duty and in the spare dwelling when on duty.

This arrangement died out as automation progressed and from November 1998 all lighthouses have been unmanned and monitored from an Operation and Planning Centre in Harwich.

LIGHTHOUSE TECHNOLOGY AND DEVELOPMENT

The lighthouse builders' skill has steadily evolved over the centuries. It achieved a high point of perfection during the Victorian era and particularly around the coast of Cornwall. The 19th century gave us the world famous Bishop Rock, Longships, Wolf Rock and Round Island stations plus the fifth Eddystone tower. In addition the lesser known stations at Trevose, Godrevy and St Anthony were erected. All were built by local labour but under the close supervision of the engineers to Trinity House who designed each structure.

Prior to the 19th century the only lights on the Cornish coast were the Eddystone, Lizard, St Agnes and the first Longships. The 20th century has seen the addition of only three more, at Pendeen and Tater Du on the mainland and Peninnis on the Isles of Scilly. This last one was to replace the old St Agnes lighthouse which was built in 1680 and no longer needed.

The most famous of the engineers involved in this 19th century programme were those of the Douglass family. Between them they built 26 towers in various parts of the world. Nicholas Douglass, born 1798, became Engineer to Trinity House after the death of James Walker who held the post before him. His two sons, James and William Douglass followed him into the Service as did his grandson William Tregarthen Douglass. Both James and William were at school in Penzance while their father was building the first tower at Bishop Rock.

But it is James, afterwards Sir James who is best remembered. In his career he was variously Assistant Engineer, Resident Engineer and finally Engineer in Chief to Trinity House. He worked on the two towers at Bishop Rock, the Smalls off the Pembrokeshire coast, the present Eddystone and the Wolf Rock. Descriptions of his work were recorded in papers read to the Institution of Civil Engineers during the 19th century and we can glean much information from them. The paper on Wolf Rock shows that he not only designed the tower and the landing platform but he also planned the work yard at Penzance, the five special barges for taking out the granite blocks to the site, the floating barrack ship for the workmen and also the special moorings needed to hold the barges close to the rock for unloading.

The first year of work at the Wolf was in 1862 and only 22 landings were possible between March and September giving just 83 hours of work on the site for the season. Sir James' description of the safety precautions needed for the early work

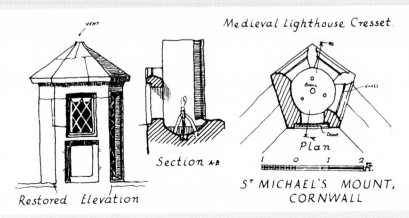

Medieval Lighthouse Cresset.

VENT

Section A-B

Plan

St MICHAEL'S MOUNT, CORNWALL

Restored Elevation

St Michael's Mount. Suggestion for original design of harbour lantern. DOUGLAS HAGUE

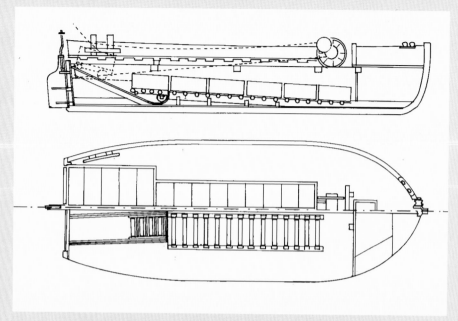

Original drawing of stone barge used at Wolf Rock. TRINITY HOUSE COLLECTION

parties digging out the foundation pit are worth recalling. Heavy stanchions were sunk in the rock and each man had a safety line within his reach. When the look out or 'crow' spotted a wave likely to sweep over the rock the men would hold on, head to the sea while it washed over them. Picks, hammers and jumpers (hand drills) were frequently swept away and lost. Each man was required to wear a cork life jacket when working on the rock and as a result there was 'no loss of life or limb to any person employed'.

All the stones were first cut and shaped in the workyard at Penzance, later the site of the Trinity House depot on the harbour. Each course of stones was then trial fitted to the one above and below it, giving rise to the popular local idea that the Wolf lighthouse was first 'erected' in Penzance. There was no inner dock then and the harbour was tidal so a special pier was constructed for loading the material into the 5 stone barges for transport to the rock. Each of these was fitted with two lines of wooden rollers in the bottom for moving the heavy granite blocks to the stern ready for lifting up to the landing platform. All hoisting was initially done by hand crane which had to be moved up the tower as it grew in height. When it had reached the 28th course of blocks it was possible to erect a steam crane which greatly speeded up the completion of the work. There are 70 courses in all from the rock to the lantern gallery.

The work of building the other isolated lighthouses off Lands End and the Isles of Scilly followed broadly similar lines as it did also for the Eddystone tower.

The land light stations were all erected by local building firms under contract to Trinity House. Arthur Carkeek of Redruth built Pendeen, Olver & Sons of Falmouth built St Anthony and Trevose while the Godrevy contract went to Thomas Eve and Thomas Williams of Helston. All these contracts included the provision of roads to the sites on the mainland, considerable work on levelling the sites and the erection of substantial walls around the premises to safeguard the Keepers and their families.

Land lighthouses are usually of fairly simple construction but have to be strong and heavy as befits their exposed position. They were all designed with a water catchment area. This could be the flat roof of the dwellings as at Pendeen or a purpose built slope as at St Anthony and Godrevy, both of which can still be seen. Nowadays of course the mainland sites are all connected to the water main.

All of these land stations originally had oil lighting apparatus installed except two. They have now been converted to electric light and take the power from the national grid with a back up generator at each one in case of mains failure. The exceptions are Tater Du which was built in 1965 so it had the advantage of electricity from the beginning and Peninnis Head. This station was built in 1911 to replace the old St Agnes lighthouse and is an un-manned station having an automatic light once acetylene lit but now electric.

St Agnes is a very good example of an early lighthouse which showed a coal fire. This was installed in 1680 when the tower was built and lasted until 1790 when oil lamps with reflectors replaced it. The brazier, or cresset, then in use still exists and is displayed on the island of Tresco. The tower of St Agnes is still standing but is now a private dwelling and not open to the public.

Dry setting the last stone on the top course of the Eddystone tower. On top (left to right) are quarry manager John Botterell, quarry masters Philips and Shearer, Sir James Douglass, Japanese attache, and resident engineer (possibly Thomas Edmond). Photographed Spring 1881 at Wadebridge setting yard of the De Lank Quarry, St Breward. AUTHOR'S COLLECTION

Although oil was used as long ago as biblical times for household illumination it was not until the late seventeen hundreds before it became a practical source of light for lighthouse purposes. Prior to that the usual light was from a coal or wood fire burning in a brazier. The only alternative being candles such as were used in the first three of the five towers built at the Eddystone.

Sometimes the fire was surrounded by a lantern but its effectiveness depended greatly on the diligence of the lightkeepers keeping the glass from being blackened in addition to their work of keeping a bright fire burning.

These lights had the further disadvantage that it was difficult to distinguish one from another. This could only be done by the added expense of providing two or more fires at a station. The present Lizard lighthouse was built in 1752 with two towers showing a fire from each. These are both still standing with one in use for the existing light. The Casquets lighthouse built in 1724 near Alderney in the Channel Islands has three towers which originally showed a fire from each. Thus the Chops of the Channel were reasonably well marked in the middle of the 18th century with a triple and a double light plus the single light at St Agnes. It was the invention of the circular wick with a current of air passing through the middle which brought lighthouse illumination out of the 'coal age'. This was invented by a Swiss, Ami Argand, in 1782 and with the addition of a glass chimney it resulted in a cleaner, brighter flame with very little smoke. Further refinements over the years to the wick raising mechanism allowed the addition of several concentric wicks in one lamp, which of course produced a much brighter light. When the present Eddystone was finished in 1882 the lamp had seven concentric wicks but the greatest number used was ten. This was done by Thomas Stevenson who was one of the famous Scottish lighthouse builders in the Victorian era, and also by James Douglass for the original optic installed at Round Island lighthouse in 1887. Fish oil was used in the early wick lamps, then vegetable oil and eventually mineral oil.

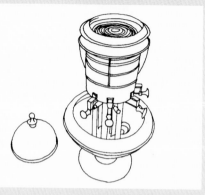

Five wick burner used at Pendeen.

Further improvements to the light source came after 1901 when Arthur Kitson invented the pressurised vapour burner. Instead of burning oil vapour at the wick it was pressurised in a retort and fed to an incandescent mantle. The retort was a small coiled copper tube above the mantle. It was first heated by a blow lamp to produce the vapour and when the mantle was lit it gave off sufficient heat to maintain a constant stream of vapour while the burner was running.

This invention had the effect of trebling

Brazier or cresset used at St Agnes prior to 1790. Now at Tresco Gardens.

the power of the light compared with the former wick burners and was another major development in lighthouse technology. One of the first to be used was in the Wolf Rock lantern but this was destroyed on modernisation of the light. These lamps and the multiple wick ones were in use until the introduction of electricity in the last forty years.

Many years prior to Kitson's work a Frenchman. Augustin Fresnel, had studied the refractive properties of glass with a view to concentrating beams of light. In I 822 he built an apparatus to be mounted in front of the light source. Before this the only enhancement of a light had been by means of a reflector placed behind it. This apparatus was a panel carrying a lens with a series of concentric prismatic rings, in segments, surrounding it. When a light was placed at the focal point of the lens a concentrated pencil beam of light was produced. He then mounted several of these panels on a carriage which he made

Lighting apparatus from St Mary's lighthouse, Northumberland.

to revolve around an oil wick burner and so invented the first flashing light from a single light source. This was the forerunner of all the magnificent optics to be found in lighthouses today.

In the early days of these flashing lights the carriage assembly ran on rollers but the friction limited the size of the assembly and also the speed at which it could revolve. Eventually in 1890 the idea of mounting the carriage on a float riding in a trough of mercury was born. This design almost eliminated the friction and allowed larger assemblies to be built and to move at greater speeds, thus increasing the diversity of light characters which could be produced. Some of the largest of this type of apparatus weigh $4^1/_2$ tons and can be pushed round by one finger. Originally they were made to revolve by means of a hand wound weight driven clock, but today it is done by a small electric motor.

Kitson Vaporised Oil Burner used at Wolf Rock (mantle is missing).

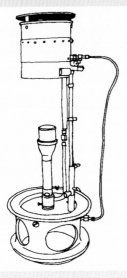

These evolutions in lighting apparatus have led to the present variety of light characters now used to distinguish one station from another:

Fixed lights – usually reserved for harbour installations.

Flashing lights – giving one or more flashes followed by longer periods of darkness during each exhibition of the character.

Occulting lights – giving long periods of

SECTOR LIGHTS

PENZANCE HARBOUR LIGHT

ST ANTHONY'S HEAD LIGHTHOUSE

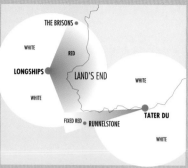

THE LAND'S END LIGHTS

light separated by short periods of darkness during each exhibition of the character.

Isophase lights – giving a long flash followed by an equal period of darkness during each exhibition of the character.

Sector lights – these are a different colour from the main light, and arranged to show over a smaller arc than it does, to identify some particular area of danger. They can be part of that main light and therefore giving the same character flash, or they may be a fixed light, usually red, which is shown from a separate, lower, window in the same tower.

Examples of the use of sectors can be found at the harbours of Newlyn, Penzance, Fowey, East Looe and Falmouth (St Anthony lighthouse) and from Godrevy lighthouse. A particularly interesting example is the Runnelstone Rock off Gwennap Head which is 'guarded' by two separate sectors. For ships approaching it from the east there is a red sector in the main (white) light of the Longships lighthouse to give them due warning, and for ships coming from the west there is a fixed red sector light shown from underneath the flashing light of the Tater Du lighthouse. Ships have of course to pass through these sectors and a prudent navigator will be giving extra care when doing so to check that he is proceeding on a safe course to clear the danger.

We have come a long way in lighthouse technology since the mariner only had a flickering coal fire to guide him.

FOG SIGNALS

In addition to the visual aids a variety of audible ones have been used over the years to assist the mariner in fog. Bells, gongs, explosives, air operated sirens and electrically operated horns have all been tried at various times. Nowadays gongs and explosives have been discontinued and bells are only used on buoys and so are whistles. Air operated sirens were once used at manned stations but now all are un-manned all fog signals are electric.

The introduction of radar on the vast majority of vessels has meant that fog signals are considered by many seafarers to be superfluous and no longer needed for navigation. The whole subject is under constant review by the governing authorities and at some stations the fog signal has already been discontinued.

WARNING FOG SIGNAL

The public are advised that a fog signal emitting a very loud noise may be sounded in this vicinity at any time without prior warning.

Trinity House   The Secretary
Tower Hill
London

Sign at Trevose Head lighthouse.
MICHAEL MESSENGER

THE CORPORATION OF TRINITY HOUSE

This is considered to be the premier lighthouse authority in the world and is certainly the oldest one. Constituted by a charter granted by King Henry VIII in 1514 with the magnificent title of The Guild, Fraternity or Brotherhood of the Most Glorious and Undivided Trinity and of Saint Clement in the Parish of Deptford Strond' it is almost the oldest institution in the United Kingdom as well. Only the Church and Parliament pre-date it.

Henry's charter was granted to a medieval Guild of Mariners although there is little historical evidence about their origin. Apparently they petitioned the King about the lack of proper control over the 'lodesmen' or pilots in the River Thames and the charter gave them general powers for the safety of shipping and effective control of pilotage.

The charter gave this control to a Master, Wardens and Assistants, who are known as Elder Brethren and comprise the Corporation of Trinity House. The head of the Service is Prince Philip, Duke of Edinburgh, known as The Master. At present two Wardens and six Assistants form the Board of Trinity House under the Chairmanship of the Deputy Master, all of whom are mariners with long experience of service at sea in the Royal or Merchant Navies, or leading figures in the world of commerce. Additionally there are currently 15 other Elder Brethren who are retired Board members or distinguished people from public life, and approximately 300 Younger Brethren who are honorary.

Trinity House has had a considerable influence on national events since it began and it is fair to say that this influence has probably shaped English history on several occasions. In 1588 the Master, Capt. Salmon, organised a fleet of 30 merchant ships to help engage the Spanish Armada. In 1632 Trinity House organised an expedition to fight the notorious Barbary Coast pirates.

In 1797 during the Mutiny at the Nore the fleet was preparing to put to sea and go over to the Dutch and French fleets which would have been a disaster for England. A party of Elder Brethren prevented this by sailing from Harwich and removing or destroying all buoys and seamarks in the Thames Estuary to the fury of

A view of Lower Hope Reach 1803–05 showing Trinity House blockships with the Trinity Yacht on the extreme right. TRINITY HOUSE COLLECTION

Trinity House depot at Penzance in 2006. ALAN KITTRIDGE

the mutineers. The full story is told in Richard Woodman's book, *Keepers of the Sea*.

In 1803 when Napoleon was threatening an invasion of England it was Trinity House who undertook to defend the Thames. They moored a flotilla of eleven frigates across the Lower Hope Reach (near Tilbury) and manned it with a body of men known as the Royal Trinity House Volunteer Artillery. This floating barricade stayed in place for over two years.

The connection with seamarks started when Queen Elizabeth the First renewed the Corporation's charter and also gave them powers to 'erect beacons, marks and signs of the sea whereby the dangers may be avoided and escaped and ships the better come into their ports without peril'. This authority however did not give them any control over the various private lighthouses then in existence nor the ones which came into being over the next 300 years.

This omission was due to the practice of the Crown issuing patents to private individuals to establish lights on payment of a rent to the Crown. In return the owners were empowered to charge fees, still known as 'light dues', to the owners of ships passing their light. They did this by appointing collectors at all the ports with authority to enquire into details of a ship's voyage and demand the requisite fee. Nowadays light dues from commercial shipping and some pleasure craft are collected by Customs and Excise acting as agents of the General Lighthouse Authorities.

It was not until 1836 that Trinity House was empowered to buy out the owners of such lighthouses and acquire full control of all those around England and Wales. The total cost for this was £1,200,000 which conveys some idea of the value of such patents to their owners. For a full description of this long episode in the history of English lighthouses one should read Douglas Hague's book.

During the 18th and 19th centuries Trinity House established their Lighthouse Service which looks after all the lighthouses, lightvessels, buoys and beacons which are in their control. Until the late 1970s these seamarks included 90 lighthouses, mostly manned ones, 30 manned lightvessels and almost 700 buoys, half of them being lighted ones. To service all these stations they had a fleet of nine lighthouse tenders, smart, efficient and purpose built ships. The original vessels in the 1800s and earlier were quite small, 60 to 80 feet long and under 100 tons, but by 1970 they were just under 2,000 tons and capable of lifting buoys weighing up to ten tons in quite poor sea conditions. These ships operated from six ports where Trinity House maintained a working depot with a single tender at five of them and four at the Harwich depot.

The Trinity House coat of arms

Cornwall had one of these Trinity House depots at Penzance, although from 2004 it has been at St Just, based at Lands End Airport. It had a very interesting history. When the decision to build the Wolf Rock lighthouse was made in 1859 it was necessary to have a base from which to conduct that operation and to carry out the reliefs of light-keepers when it was completed. Penzance was the obvious choice to site this base although at that time it had only an open foreshore i.e. tidal, and protected by the South pier and Albert pier. The site chosen contained a warehouse, blacksmith's shop and yard, and a dwelling house. It was leased by Trinity House for 14 years at an annual rent of £100 and was on the foreshore, just above high water mark. On completion of the lighthouse the premises were purchased and subsequently converted for use as a buoy maintenance yard and a base for conducting the reliefs of the off shore lighthouses in the area and the Seven Stones lightvessel.

For long after Penzance had a very close affinity with the Trinity House Corporation, providing most of the crews of the various tenders stationed there and the lightvessel crew plus many of the lightkeepers for Cornish lighthouses. Shortly after the depot was completed it became an annual occurrence for the Town's Regatta committee to ask for the loan of the Trinity House tender to use as their Committee boat. The request was always granted as the Minute Books at Trinity House show and this happy relationship continued until the 1900s.

Sadly the historical link with the town has been very much weakened by the changes which have occurred in the manning scales of the Lighthouse Service. Although the harbour is used occasionally most transport offshore is by helicopter. The depot had a new lease of life as the National Lighthouse Centre, with a fascinating display of lighthouse engineering and artifacts, but that, sadly, closed in 2004.

Trinity House Master's flag

Trinity House ensign

Trinity House jack

BEACONS, MARKS AND SIGNS OF THE SEA

When those words were written into the charter given to Trinity House by Elizabeth I no one could have foreseen the array of nautical 'sign posts' that we now have. Beside the well known lighthouses and lightvessels with their distinctive flashing lights and raucous fog horns we have an assortment of buoys, lighted and unlighted, beacons and daymarks. Each buoy has its own 'character' which is a distinctive combination of shape, colour, light flash and top mark (sometimes called a daymark) depending on its position and function. Whether it marks a wreck or a channel, a 'safe water' area, a water ski area, the end of a sewer outfall pipe or a practice bombing area the mariner should be able to read its character, identify its purpose and plot his course accordingly.

Beacons or daymarks, since they are not lighted and only usable in daylight are mostly used for marking isolated rocks which can provide a firm base for their erection. Although more expensive to establish they are much cheaper to maintain than a buoy with moorings which need regular inspection and overhaul. They often served a secondary function in the work of the Trinity House tenders when checking floating seamarks in the vicinity. Being easily identifiable as well as being accurately marked on a chart they were used to obtain horizontal sextant angles or compass bearings to plot the position of a buoy or a sunken wreck in the same area. Nowadays this task is done by using electronic aids.

When lightvessels were first introduced they nearly all carried a large daymark at the top of the mast, sometimes two. They could be shaped like a globe, cone, square, hourglass (two cones point to point) or even a Saint Andrew's Cross. This meant easier identification in poor visibility, especially in the Thames estuary where several lightvessels were within sight of each other. It also allowed sailing ships to sight them at long range and so avoid the need to get close enough to read the name on their side. These

Gribben Head daymark was sold to the National Trust for £1 but continues to serve as a daymark.
GORDON HILL

Gribben daymark doorway plaque. ALAN KITTRIDGE

daymarks have been discontinued since the Second World War with the introduction of radio aids.

Sometimes two beacons are erected ashore, one higher than the other, so that they can be seen from seaward when in line. This line may indicate a safe channel to be followed or can be set to cross an off shore danger as in the case of the dangerous Runnelstone rock off Gwennap Head in Penwith. These two beacons were erected ashore a mile away in 1821. They are both 12 feet high, the rear one is conical, painted black and white while the front, lower one is a red pyramid.

There are two more pairs of these ancient beacons on the Lizard peninsular, sited so that, when viewed from seaward, the two lines cross where the submerged rocks known as the Vrogue lie. The most prominent daymark in Cornwall is on Gribben Head in St Austell Bay.

Runnelstone beacons. ALAN KITTRIDGE

It was erected in 1832 and is 84 feet high, painted in red and white bands. It was put up to distinguish the headland from its neighbours Dodman and St Anthony. It thus assisted sailing ships to find the ports of Fowey, Par or Charlestown without having to close the coast too soon.

Another prominent daymark exists at Portreath and is now a Scheduled Monument. Details are listed later in the book. Although lighthouses have a special place in the affections of the public, for many reasons, the role of the lightvessel as a nautical signpost is equally important. It performs the same function as the former but it is used in places where it would be impossible to build a tower. The majority of these are on the east coast of England where the dangerous sandbanks offer no solid foundation but there is one famous lightvessel on the Cornish coast. This marks the notorious Seven Stones reef between Lands End and Scilly. A survey showed that the rock was unsuitable for building on and the station was established in 1841 after a long history of wrecks occurring on the reef. One of the worst of these was *HMS Lizard* lost in February 1747 with 100 men aboard.

The reef had such a wicked reputation that coasting ships frequently went to the westward of the Scillies when rounding Lands End if the weather was such that they could not hug the land. The most famous wreck that occurred here was the Torrey Canyon on 18 March 1967. She ran aground in broad daylight and caused the most serious oil pollution incident ever experienced in our waters.

The Seven Stones lightvessel is in the most exposed position of any around the British coast and in consequence has broken adrift from her mooring on several occasions. This mooring now consists of 300 fathoms of heavy chain with links one and three-quarter inches thick and a four ton anchor on the end. Before automation she carried two spare cables each with an anchor, As a result on each occasion of breaking adrift the crew have re-anchored her with no difficulty.

Since 1987 this station has been un-manned and fully automatic as regards light and fog signal.

Sevenstones lightvessel. NORMAN FITKIN

THE RELIEF

For the men who used to man our lightvessels and the off shore lighthouses the word 'relief' had a very special significance. That was the day when the crew or the keepers were relieved and according to whether a man was 'going off' or 'coming off' so he felt depressed or elated.

Prior to 1970 in Cornish waters this relief day could be a fixed or moveable date according to the station concerned. For the Seven Stones and Round Island, which were not subject to very long bad weather delays the relief pattern was a fixed cycle. It fell due on a Tuesday at four week intervals. On that day one half of the crew were changed over and fresh food was delivered for the men who were halfway through their eight week stint. Any delay caused by bad weather had to be accepted – swings and roundabouts – and it did not affect the following relief day. This would fall exactly four weeks later, the 28 day cycle.

For the other stations in the Penzance group of reliefs, Wolf Rock, Longships, Bishop Rock and Eddystone there was a 29 day cycle to take account of the very long delays which could sometimes occur. This 29 days started on the day that the relief was actually accomplished and meant that the next relief would be due 28 days from the day after a man stepped on shore. This of course made life very difficult for the keepers and their families. They could never plan any holiday activity until the man actually stepped ashore to start his 28 days off duty. It was quite common for delays to occur, a week or ten days was nothing unusual in wintertime and many longer delays are well documented.

Of these four lighthouses by far the worst, in terms of conditions which surrounded the relief, was the Wolf. The other three were relieved by a local

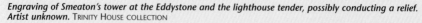

Engraving of Smeaton's tower at the Eddystone and the lighthouse tender, possibly conducting a relief. Artist unknown. Trinity House collection

Wolf Rock. RNLI lifeboat waiting to carry out relief and signalling to keepers. AUTHOR'S COLLECTION

contractor, who was an experienced boatman living in the vicinity of each i.e. at Sennen, St Mary's or Plymouth. This meant that a man due to go off to his station could be at home if the weather was bad while waiting for the boatman to judge when the conditions were right to go out. But the Wolf was always relieved by the lighthouse tender stationed at Penzance and the keepers going on duty joined her there. He often had to live on board while she waited for a favourable landing and perhaps spent the time performing other work on the District in more sheltered waters.

If this keeper was a poor sailor he could have a very miserable period of sea sickness while waiting for the austere comfort of his stone prison. He had the added misery of knowing that the delay he was enduring could easily be repeated in 29 days time. So his eight week tour of duty could sometimes be extended three times, ie. when first going off, at the middle of the half-turn relief and again when he was due to finish. It was well known for a man to be away for 12 weeks all told instead of the expected eight and there are several who suffered 14 or 15 weeks continuous duty in a really bad winter.

One has to remember that lighthouse keepers are not seamen and so the process of getting ashore at one of those isolated pillar lights could be a real ordeal. Passage

to the lighthouse landing was in a small boat, either from the tender or in the one used by the local contractor. A keeper would be apprehensive about it if the sea was rough and extremely nervous about being lifted out at the station. This was by means of a small hand crane having a rope with a loop at the end.

Before the introduction of the helicopter visitors or keepers all arrived via the hand crane at the Wolf Rock. AUTHOR'S COLLECTION

The Trinity House tender STELLA relieving the Sevenstones lightvessel. NORMAN FITKIN

He had to put one foot in this loop and cling on to the rope. If the two keepers manning the crane were slow in lifting him out as the boat rose on a wave he could easily be bounced on the gunwale or, worse still, dunked in the sea after leaving the boat. That meant he was very wet on reaching the landing but he immediately had to take over one of the winch handles and help to lift his 'opposite number' down into the boat. When all the lifting had been done – men, stores, food or luggage – he then had to strip the crane down and pull it up into the lighthouse for safe stowage before he could unpack and find some dry clothes. It was no place for the faint hearted.

Today that scene is quite different and is only a lingering memory to people in the Service. None of the Cornish off-shore stations are manned and the old pattern of reliefs is all but forgotten. The few isolated ones left elsewhere on the English coast were all automated by November 1998. The only visitors to the Cornish ones now are the electricians and engineers to maintain the equipment and their stay is usually quite brief. Attendants from the St Just depot accompany them and deal with the routine of re-filling the oil and water tanks during the same visit by means of 100 gallon rubber bags slung beneath the helicopter.

Boats from the STELLA at Longships lighthouse
AUTHOR'S COLLECTION

The lighhouse keeper's life has often been depicted as glamorous or dramatic but this was not a true picture. It was really one of great monotony only rarely interrupted by anything unusual and has been aptly described as 'like living in a lamp post'. The routine of each station was established many years ago and followed a set watch-keeping pattern which ensured that one man was always awake.

At night the keeper's duty consisted in checking that the light was exhibited correctly and watching for signs of fog. When the rotation of the lens was controlled by a descending weight this had to be wound up by hand at frequent intervals. No mean task since it weighed well over one hundredweight. This manual operation has been replaced by an electric motor for twenty years or more. During daylight hours he had routine checks to make on station machinery and equipment, weather reports to make, plus cleaning windows and brass work. In the event of any mishap all three of the keepers would be available for work.

At land stations the keepers work is very similar and also includes showing visitors around the station but no such pleasant interlude occurred at a rock station. In Victorian times visitors were allowed at the island stations, Godrevy, Round Island and Plymouth Breakwater but this was discontinued about the time of the Great War and never resumed. Since then the keepers at all rock lighthouses have only had the company of the other two keepers and it was always something of a lottery whether they were all compatible. In the close confines of their voluntary imprisonment the most innocent habit can become unbearable. Sniffing, stirring your tea in a noisy manner or simply not washing up properly could lead to real antagonism.

Although the living quarters in a lighthouse tower are adequate they are far from being very congenial. Each man has a separate bunk in the same bedroom but they are naturally curved to fit the circular room and were never really comfortable for a tall man. They are aptly named 'banana bunks'. Only in the Round Island station is there space enough for men to have a separate room with a proper bed.

On the pillar lighthouses there is very little space for obtaining exercise. The greatest distance one can actually walk in a straight line is about 12 feet across the living room and that is after the chairs and table have been moved to allow it to be done. Running up and down the circular stairs can provide exercise of course but is a very boring way to do it.

Each man was responsible for

Cleaning the lantern house on the Eddystone.
AUTHOR'S COLLECTION

Tea time at Wolf Rock. A communal teapot but each man has his own tin of milk. TRINITY HOUSE COLLECTION

obtaining his own food and for cooking it. This was a hallowed tradition in lighthouse life and ensured that a man had what he liked, not something that an unknown catering supply officer thought might be suitable. Usually the men ran a common mess for their main meal to reduce the work of cooking but there was no compulsion to do so other than that of 'common usage and practice'.

Washing arrangements were very primitive in the pillar lighthouses being confined to the kitchen sink. If a man wanted a bath he had to stand in a bucket, one foot at a time, and try not to make too much mess.

Sanitary facilities were equally sparse, consisting of another bucket in the lantern room, which was emptied over the gallery rail. A new keeper quickly learned to tell which was the 'lee side' and found a deeper meaning in the phrase 'getting your own back'. There was also an old paint tin kept in the window recess outside the bedroom for overnight use. This window was always easy to identify from outside because of the long stain below it on the stonework.

Life on the Seven Stones lightvessel was similar in some respects to a lighthouse keeper's but by no means all. To begin with the crew were all seamen whereas the keepers were landsmen and there were more of them on board.

In the last century she carried 11 men but this was reduced to seven between the wars and to five since the 1960s. The senior man was always known as the Master.

There were two reasons for having 11 men in the beginning. The ship is moored in very deep water and her cable had to be hove short at frequent intervals to make sure it did not become foul of her own anchor. As this work was done with a hand windlass the extra men were needed to assist with this very essential work. In addition to this it was sometimes necessary, before the advent of radio, to send the pulling boat away to assist a ship in distress on the reef and this also required extra man-power.

There was a watch keeping routine on board as there was on the lighthouses but in addition a proper look-out was required to watch for any ship which might approach too close and endanger the lightvessel. For the seamen the most irksome part of their life on board was the fact that the ship was always at anchor and never went anywhere. In bad weather they would see other ships making for harbour but had to remain on station themselves and ride out whatever came their way.

Until refrigerators were introduced to the lighthouse service after the last war it was a difficult problem to ensure that one's food lasted from one relief to the next. Salt meat and salt fish were used from the beginning of the Service, followed by tinned food when this came into general use. Tinned milk was of course essential, as was the ability to make your own bread.

Sometimes a man would preserve fresh meat by cooking it slowly, cutting it up and packing it in jars sealed with mutton fat.

Catching fresh fish was easy enough from the lightvessel of course and occasionally from the island lighthouses in fine weather. But the really ingenious method used on the isolated pillar lights was kite fishing from the lantern gallery 120 feet above the sea. For this a man would make his own kite, about five or six feet tall, with a very long tail which carried the baited hook. The idea was to get this hook into the water on the outside edge of the rocks where the fish were feeding.

It required a great deal of skill to launch the kite and fly it out, rather than up, but low enough to keep the hook submerged. As soon as a fish was hooked, which could easily be a four or five pounder, the extra weight made the kite shoot up, lifting the catch quite high. More skill was then needed to play the kite so that one could grab the tail, remove the fish and still keep it flying ready for the next cast. It

was said that a really skilled fisherman could bring the kite in so that the fish would be hanging just level with the kitchen window three floors below. A quick tap on the flue pipe from the stove which came up beside the lantern would alert the cook of the day to reach out of the window and retrieve the fresh supply. A real 'fisherman's tale'!

Wake up call on the Eddystone. Author'scollection

THE LIGHTHOUSE SERVICE TODAY

In recent years a great deal has been heard about the programme of Lighthouse Automation but automatic lighthouses have been with us for many years. Peninnis Head in the Isles of Scilly was an automatic light, controlled by a sun valve, from its very beginning in 1911. Godrevy lighthouse began as a manned station in 1859 but became automatic in 1934 when an acetylene light was installed. Tater Du lighthouse, the last Cornish one to be built, was automatic from the start of its life in 1965.

What is new of course is the sophisticated remote control apparatus used to monitor the performance of the major lighthouse and lightvessel stations and to control them with nobody on board. The first one to be unmanned and remotely controlled was the Eddystone in 1982, exactly 100 years after it was erected. This station was first monitored from Penlee Point, at the entrance to Plymouth Sound, where a direct line of sight was possible, a necessary requirement for equipment using UHF radio. Since then the great increase in radio traffic generally has led Trinity House to adopt microwave radio links to cope with the increased number of automated stations in the South West. The Eddystone was re-engineered in 1999 to solar power control and, like all others, is now monitored from Harwich. The initial increase in the number of monitoring stations coupled with the expanded use of the helicopter to attend to maintenance or casualty work allowed Trinity House to institute a full programme of automation of all their manned lighthouses and lightvessels. The programme has now reached its conclusion as regards both the off-shore establishments around Cornwall and the shore establishments. The monitoring of these latter is less expensive as it is done over a normal telephone line.

Trinity House have calculated that the cost of automation of a typical lighthouse is approximately £365,000 and the savings that will be made will pay this back in four or five years. The savings will come principally from dispensing with the crews but other savings will be made on their transport costs, heating, lighting and consumable stores together with the cost of providing family accommodation at most of the land stations.

The overall consideration is to reduce the cost of the lighthouse service to the people who pay for it without reducing its efficiency. Those who pay are the shipowners through the light dues levied on their ships. Since they also pay for the very sophisticated navigation equipment on those ships it is understandable that some are reluctant to fund any lighthouse expenditure which is not fully justifiable. In the Cornish area all off-shore stations were fully automated by 1992 and all land stations by 1998, as was the rest of Britain.

One other very significant alteration in the Lighthouse Service in recent years has been the great decrease in the fleet of tenders needed. The nine in service at the end of the Second World War were reduced to five in 1973 almost concurrent with the start of the programme to equip all lightvessels and the off-shore lighthouses with helicopter pads. This programme has now come to an end but the helicopter itself was introduced even before the first pad was finished, where-ever personnel could be winched on and off their station. The expansion since then in the use of this versatile machine has meant a steady decline in the work load of the tenders, despite the recent removal of helipads from lightvessels.

First came the introduction of helicopter reliefs of personnel followed by the replenishment of water and oil by the use of underslung loads carried in 100 gallon rubber bags. As a result the traditional lighthouse work of the tenders has virtually

Trinity House helicopter and Longships lighthouse with a helipad, in a storm. AUTHOR'S COLLECTION

disappeared and they are now only concerned with buoy maintenance and work in connection with light vessel moorings and with wreck marking. There are now only two ships left in the fleet with a third held in reserve in case of damage to either of them.

Much has been said about the removal of lighthouse keepers and the adverse effect this might have on the safety of people and ships in distress. However it was never a requirement in the lighthouse service for a keeper to maintain a constant look out. His job was to maintain the navigational aids at his station. He would of course respond to any request from the coastguard service to keep a lookout for some overdue yacht or fishing vessel but Merchant Shipping legislation only requires the lighthouse service to provide the aids to navigation. Other organisations are charged with the safety of life requirement.

The extensive alteration to the work of Trinity House should be seen as simply the latest step in its long history. Each advance in technology, better lighting, better fog signals, new radio aids, better tenders, helicopter use and now automation has been introduced to improve the service given to seafarers. Queen Elizabeth the First would surely be very proud of their 'beacons, marks and signs of the sea'.

Captain Michael Tarrant aboard the Trinity House tender STELLA.
NORMAN FITKIN

CAPTAIN MICHAEL TARRANT
1922-2003

Michael Tarrant joined Trinity House as an apprentice in 1939 and enjoyed a very commendable career until he retired in 1983 as District Superintendent of the South Coast. During that time he commanded a number of Trinity House vessels, including the flagship *Patricia*. He rescued the gale-stricken East Goodwin Lightship in 1961 and in 1965 salvaged the Greek freighter *Nymphaia* after a mid-channel collision. For some five years he was in command of the *Stella* based at Penzance and responsible for servicing some of the most difficult and famous lighthouses around the British coast. In retirement he returned to Penzance and took an active role in the Trevithick Society. It is fitting that this book, which was his first, written in 1990, should deal with the lighthouses and vessels with which he was so familiar.

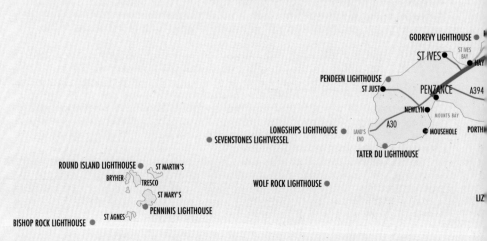

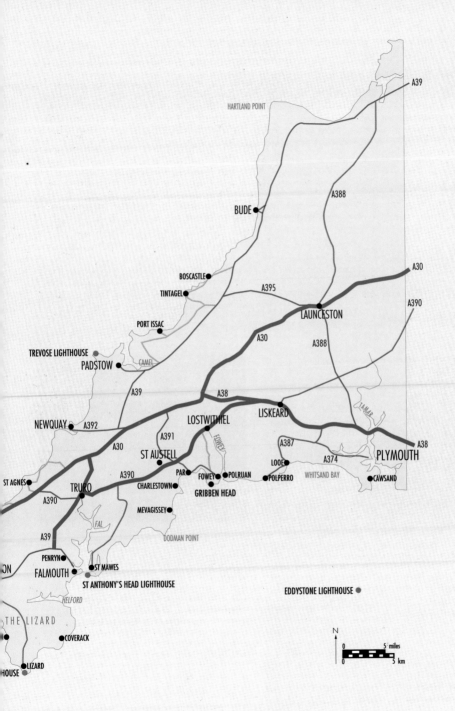

HARTLAND POINT

A39

A388

BUDE

BOSCASTLE
TINTAGEL
A395
A30

A30

A390

LAUNCESTON

PORT ISSAC
A388

TREVOSE LIGHTHOUSE
PADSTOW
CAMEL

A39
A38

NEWQUAY
A392
LOSTWITHIEL
LISKEARD

TAMAR

A30
LOSTWITHIEL
A391
A38
PLYMOUTH

ST AGNES
ST AUSTELL
A387
LOOE
A374
WHITSAND BAY
CAWSAND

TRURO
A390
PAR
FOWEY
POLRUAN
POLPERRO

A390
CHARLESTOWN
GRIBBEN HEAD

FAL
MEVAGISSEY

A39
DODMAN POINT

PENRYN
FALMOUTH
ON
ST MAWES
ST ANTHONY'S HEAD LIGHTHOUSE

HELFORD

THE LIZARD

COVERACK
EDDYSTONE LIGHTHOUSE

LIZARD
HOUSE

N

0   5 miles
0   5 km

All lighthouses are privately owned by Trinity House except for the minor ones marking harbour entrances which belong to the local authority. None of them are public property and it is a misconception that visitors have an automatic right of admission because they are taxpayers. The money to fund the lighthouse service comes from the Light Dues paid by ships entering or leaving our ports and not from the payment of taxes or rates.

The lighthouses at Lizard Point and Pendeen have been open in the past and it is Trinity House's intention to have Visitor Centres at each during the summer months. Times are variable and it is best to check locally or on the Trinity House website for opening times and admission charges.

Now that they are no longer used by keepers it is possible to rent holiday cottages at St Anthony, Pendeen, Trevose Head and the Lizard.

In the details of station characteristics listed for each lighthouse the term 'candle power' to denote the intensity of a light has been replaced with the international one 'candela'. The range of a light is the distance at which it can be seen on a dark night with a clear atmosphere. It depends on the intensity of the light and also the height of it above sea level.

The foolowing guide is arranged in geographical order around the coast, running down the north coast to Lands End, around the Isles of Scilly, and along the south coast towards Plymouth.

TREVOSE HEAD LIGHTHOUSE
[SW 850770]
Situated on the north coast of Cornwall about 4 1/2 miles from Padstow and signposted from the village of St Merryn. The final half mile of the road is through private property and a toll is payable. This station was built by Jacob and Thomas Olver of Falmouth in 1847 after many shipwrecks on the coast and almost as many petitions to Trinity House for a lighthouse to be built. When first lit it showed two fixed white lights and there was no fog signal. Since this did not

Trevose Head. GORDON HILL

Trevose, showing the enormous Rayleigh's trumpet foghorn, removed after 1964. AUTHOR'S COLLECTION

involve very much work for the men the complement was fixed at two keepers.

In 1882 the station was modernised, the light was altered to a single white occulting one and the complement of keepers increased to three. Since then a further alteration on 1 August 1912 changed the light to a flashing red one.

At the same time Lord Rayleigh, who was then scientific adviser to Trinity House erected an experimental fog signal at the station. This had an enormous horn, 36 feet long, rectangular in shape, and the

Trevose Head lighthouse. MICHAEL MESSENGER

mouth of it was 18 feet high by two feet wide. It was nicknamed 'Rayleigh's Trumpet' and was in use from 1913 until replaced in 1964.

The station was automated in 1995 and the red light changed to white

STATION CHARACTERISTICS:

Light: one white flash every 7.5 seconds, intensity 136,000 candela, range 21 miles.

Fog signal: electric, giving two blasts every 30 seconds.

GODREVY LIGHTHOUSE

[SW 578437]

Standing on Godrevy Island in St Ives Bay this lighthouse is a guide for vessels bound for Hayle and provides a warning of the Stones, a dangerous reef which extends seawards from the island for a mile and a half. It was also a most useful 'passing' light for ships sailing between Lands End and the Bristol Channel in the days when prudent seafarers took compass bearings of coastal lights to obtain a 'fix' on their position.

The reef and the island claimed many lives and countless wrecks including the passenger steamer *Nile* wrecked in December 1854 with all hands. This disaster led to pressure from the public and from seafaring interests for Trinity House to establish a light in the area. After considerable debate about whether to erect it on the island or on the reef itself

work started on the island in 1858. The white octagonal tower is made of rubble stone bedded in mortar and stands 86 feet high. It took just over a year to build at a cost of £7,082.15s.7d and the light was first shown on 1 March 1859. There was a cottage for the keepers and the remains of it are still to be seen. The original optic was a revolving one driven by a clock operated by a weight running down a cavity in the wall. There was also a fixed red light below the main light which showed over an arc of 44 degrees to mark the Stones reef. This arc is now covered by a red sector in the main light itself. A fog bell was also fitted which sounded one stroke every five seconds.

The main lighting apparatus was originally purchased several years earlier for use at the Bishop Rock when the first, iron, tower had been started. This was

Godrevy Island. GORDON HILL

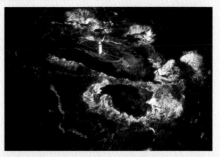

Godrevy lighthouse. MICHAEL MESSENGER

washed away before the light was installed.

The lighthouse was first manned by three keepers with only two on station at any one time. An unhappy incident many years later caused this complement to be increased to four, with three on station at a time. This happened when one man was taken ill at Christmas 1925 and was brought ashore by lifeboat. A relief keeper could not be landed for a week and his companion remained in sole occupation, a matter of great concern to Trinity House who decreed that all stations should be manned by three keepers in future. In 1934 the station was down-graded to the status of an automatic, unwatched one. The revolving light was then replaced by one having a fixed lens surrounding a flashing light using acetylene gas. At the same time the fog bell was discontinued.

All routine maintenance and repairs are effected by landing men from a helicopter. The island has become a favourite nesting place for sea birds and in the breeding season it is quite usual to see them sifting on nests near the landing pad screaming defiance at the whirling blades just over their heads.

One curious and almost forgotten feature at this lighthouse was a small aerial ropeway linking the main island to the small one on the southern side across the narrow channel between them. This small one had a landing place which was sometimes accessible to a boat when the two landings on the main island were not. The link was provided by a taut wire carrying a 'traveller' between two stout posts across the gap. A strong lightweight chair was suspended from it and the occupant pulled himself across by an endless rope running in a pulley block on

Wire rope span at Godrevy. Its use was probably discontinued in the 1920s with the introduction of a motor boat for relieving the keepers.

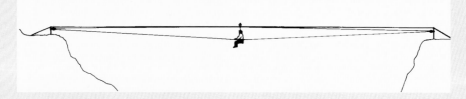

Godrevy in 1978. The experimental wind generator was not a success and the lattice tower no longer exists. Author's collection

each post. The chair was still in existence at the station in 1942 although the rest of the equipment had been removed some years earlier

Pendeen lighthouse. Alan Kittridge

Station characteristics:
Light: now solar powered, flashing white/red every ten seconds. Red sector visible between 101 and 145 degrees. Intensity 4,370/817 candela, range 12/9 miles.
Fog signal: none.

PENDEEN LIGHTHOUSE
[SW 379359]
Standing less than two miles from Pendeen village on the headland known as Pendeen Watch this lighthouse came surprisingly late into Cornwall's lighthouse story. No one knows just how many ships and lives were lost on that bleak stretch of coast between Lands End and St Ives Bay before the light was established in 1900. Suffice it to say that it has earned its keep many times over since then although it has rarely, if ever, provided any dramatic news stories as the Wolf and Bishop have done.

The station was built by Arthur Carkeek of Redruth to a design prepared by Trinity House. It was constructed of rubble stone coated internally and externally with cement mortar. The dwellings have flat roofs originally designed as water catchments for the occupants as does the separate engine house to provide cooling water for the air compressors to operate the fog signal.

The original lens apparatus, weighing 2½ tons and floating in a trough of mercury is still in use but the light source has changed. It was originally an oil lamp with five concentric wicks and is now preserved. In 1926 mains electricity was connected to the station and the light was converted to an electric one with a stand-by generator in the engine house in case of mains failure.

This light has a curious relationship with the one at Trevose nearly 40 miles along the coast. On a clear dark night a keeper on watch in the lantern can just see the light from Trevose but only at low water. Apparently the earth's curvature between the two places is just sufficient for the rising tide to obscure it from his view. Open to the public as a visitor centre.

STATION CHARACTERISTICS:
Light: four white flashes every 15 seconds, range 16 miles, intensity 150,000 candela.
Fog signal: electric, giving one blast every 20 seconds.

SEVEN STONES LIGHT VESSEL

The nautical position for this station is latitude 50 degrees 03.58 north, longitude 6 degrees 04.28 west which is 15 miles

A very early lightvessel in use between the two World Wars, showing the six feet diameter daymark at the masthead. The lantern was lowered every day for the crew to attend to the cluster of oil lamps inside; refilling with oil, trimming wicks, cleaning reflectors and glazing. GIBSON COLLECTION

WNW of the Longships lighthouse off Lands End. The light is clearly visible at night from the mainland but in daylight it needs a good pair of binoculars to pick out this fairly small ship even on a very clear day. It is about the size of a large trawler, 133 feet long and 19 feet beam. It carries one mast and the light is shown from a lantern mounted in a tower amidships.

The Sevenstones lighvessel pictured from the Trinity House vessel STELLA. NORMAN FITKIN

The helicopter landing pad on the stern was removed by 2005. It is now fully automatic with no crew on board and its performance is monitored from the mainland as are the un-manned lighthouses in the area. The navigation light on all un-manned stations is kept alight for the whole 24 hours and this will assist to identify the lightvessel from the mainland when sighted.

Most of the original accommodation and storage space has been stripped out and the spaces filled with foam which should ensure that the ship remains afloat in the event of collision damage. The ship is still moored to a four ton anchor by very heavy duty chain, and regular inspections by one of the Trinity House tenders are made to check the wear which occurs as the chain drags over the sand and rocks on the sea bed when the ship swings with the wind and tide.

On these occasions the fuel oil tanks are replenished and also the fresh water which is kept on board for the use of visiting engineers and electricians when carrying out routine maintenance. The ship has been unmanned since 1987 which demonstrates how effective the automation work has been.

STATION CHARACTERISTICS:
Light: three white flashes every 30 seconds. Visible 23 miles. Hull painted red.
Fog horn: three blasts every 60 seconds.

The first Longships lighthouse built in 1995 and replaced in 1873. AUTHOR'S COLLECTION

LONGSHIPS LIGHTHOUSE
[SW 320253]
The present tower at this station is the second one to be built here. Situated 1¼ miles 292 degrees from Lands End it is built on Carn Bras. This is the largest of a group of small islands called Longships because of a fancied resemblance to a fleet of such craft. The first tower was built

Longships lighthouse. NORMAN FITKIN

Wreck of the SS BLUEJACKET on the Longships.
F E GIBSON

privately by a Lieutenant Henry Smith under a licence granted by Trinity House. It was completed in 1795 and he was to pay a rent of £100 per year for 50 years while at the same time he could collect the light dues from ships which had passed the lighthouse. Soon afterwards he was declared incapable of managing the station and Trinity House took it over.

This tower was only 40 feet tall and stood on the highest part of the rock 40 feet above sea level. In consequence its light was often obscured by heavy seas breaking over it and damage occurred on a number of occasions. Eventually it was decided to build a bigger tower which was done between 1870 and 1873 and this was erected alongside the first one which was afterwards demolished. The decision to replace it was a timely one as in 1874 the rock on which it had been standing split away and slid into the sea.

When this station was manned the relief was carried out by a boatman living in Sennen Cove and the keepers' families lived in a row of cottages on the cliff top at Lands End. These are still standing but are now privately owned since the station is no longer manned. It was from the upper windows of these cottages that the keepers' wives used to semaphore messages to their husbands on the lighthouse. He could send one in return by standing in front of the lighthouse door. The door and its surrounding frame were painted white to provide a better background and this can still clearly be seen from the cliffs at Lands End. A telescope was required of course for each message to be read by the recipient.

Perhaps the most famous wreck which occurred here was the steam ship *Bluejacket* which, on a clear night, ran on to rocks close to the lighthouse on 10 November 1898. All 22 of the crew were saved by the Sennen lifeboat.

The light was provided by Argand oil lamps in the first lighthouse and was a fixed one, i.e. not flashing. When the second tower was erected the lighting apparatus was changed to a pressure vapour lamp with incandescent mantles. At the same time the character was altered to isophase — a long period of light followed by an equal period of darkness. This was achieved by lowering a cylinder over the lamp to black it out since it was impossible to keep switching an oil lamp on and off to obtain such a character.

In 1967 the station was modernised and an electric light was installed. Since then it has been altered to automatic operation and the keepers have been removed. It became solar powered in 2005.

STATION CHARACTERISTICS:

Light: Isophase every ten seconds, white to seaward and red to landward covering the Brisons, the inside passage, and the Runnelstone rock. Range 18 miles. Intensity 40,500 candela.

Fog signal: one blast every ten seconds.

Longships lighthouse. AUTHOR'S COLLECTION

Wolf Rock lighthouse. NORMAN FITKIN

WOLF ROCK LIGHTHOUSE

Lying 820 miles 226 degrees from Lands End [SW 342254] this dangerous rock was the graveyard for innumerable ships until it was marked by the tower built between 1862 and 1870. Prior to that several attempts were made to establish a beacon between 1795 and 1850 but all except the last one were quickly demolished by the sea.

The origin of the name Wolf has caused some speculation in recent years some of it quite fanciful. It was variously called Gulf, Gulfe, or Gulph on old maps as far back as 1576 which may simply be a corruption of the word engulf. This in turn would easily be converted into 'Wolf by common usage. It is also suggested that it was a mis-spelling of the old Cornish world 'gwelva' meaning 'viewpoint' or 'something to look out for'. What is crystal clear to any seafarer is that the name has nothing whatever to do with the sound of a wolf howling being produced by the wind blowing through a crevice in the rock! If such a thing was even remotely possible it is quite certain that the sound could never be heard above the noise of breaking waves and the sound of the wind tormenting the rigging of a sailing ship.

The rock is surrounded by water 20 fathoms deep on all sides except on the south-east where a shoal extends which only carries five fathoms over it. Elsewhere the 20 fathoms depth rapidly increases to 34 fathoms within a mile. Since it is fully exposed to the Atlantic Ocean it receives a tremendous pounding in bad weather and even in good conditions there is often a swell rolling over it.

The task of building a lighthouse on it

Wolf Rock taken by a RAF patrol from St Mawgan.

Wolf Rock lighthouse. AUTHOR'S COLLECTION

thick and this gradually decreases to 2 feet 3 inches at the narrowest part near the top.

The entrance door is made of gun-metal and is in two halves with a total weight of one ton. Curiously they are hinged to open inwards which might be considered a weakness when resisting the pounding of a heavy sea. But this is not the case since the greatest force the door is required to combat is the suction caused by heavy masses of water falling down past it. The actual weight of the breaking wave is received by the solid part of the tower below the door. In heavy weather a breaking sea is flung upwards with immense power and easily reaches the lantern itself. At night this curtain of white water rising outside will suddenly reflect the lighthouse beam of light back into the lantern room and can be a very frightening sight for a new keeper.

must have seemed very daunting from the very first landing by the builder, James Douglass, on 1 July 1861. His purpose then was to survey the rock and select a site for the tower but after a short period the swell began to increase and he had to be hauled back to the boat through the surf by a line tied round his waist. Such an occurrence proved to be quite frequent during the subsequent work of building. This commenced on 17 March 1862 and there were only 22 landings made in that first season.

The work of building this tower was conducted from a work-yard located on the foreshore at Penzance where the former Trinity House depot stood. All the stone blocks used in its construction were cut and shaped here and trial fitted to each other. So accurate was this work that none of them needed any alteration after leaving the yard. The total weight of the granite used in this tower was 3,297 tons and a further 1,078 tons was needed for the landing platform.

The height of this lighthouse is 116$\frac{1}{2}$ feet to the lantern galley and it is solid for the first 39 feet except for a space which forms the water tank.

The walls at the entrance door are 7 feet 9$\frac{1}{2}$ inches

The last stone of the tower was laid on 19 July 1869 and afterwards the lantern was installed ready for the light to be exhibited for the first time on 1 January 1870. When first installed the light was an oil burning one until converted to electricity in 1955 by the installation of diesel generators. This tower was the first lighthouse in the world to have a helicopter landing platform fitted above the lantern. It is now solar powered .

STATION CHARACTERISTICS:

Light: one white flash every 15 seconds, intensity 378,000 candela, range 23 miles.
Fog signal: Nautophone giving one blast every 30 seconds.

ROUND ISLAND LIGHTHOUSE
[SV 902178]

Erected 2$\frac{1}{2}$ miles north of St Mary's, Isles of Scilly, this lighthouse occupies a small island of the same name. It was built at the same time that the Bishop was being strengthened and was finished in 1887. St Agnes lighthouse was still in use so this third station completed the ring of warning lights around this cluster of highly dangerous islands.

The height of the tower is only 46 feet up to the lantern gallery but standing on the

Round Island lighthose clock.
AUTHOR'S COLLECTION

Round Island lighthouse. NORMAN FITKIN

top of the island 180 feet above the sea it has a most commanding position. When first built it was provided with an aerial hoist to bring relief supplies up from the boat, including of course the coal, oil and fresh water needed by the keepers. This hoist became redundant when the helicopter took over the task of landing stores and it was removed during the 1970s. Another piece of the original equipment which sadly has disappeared is the magnificent bi-form lens apparatus which was 15 feet tall and weighed over eight tons. It was in fact a twin of the one installed in the Bishop tower two years earlier which is still in use. The Round Island light source was more powerful than the Bishop however, being a ten wick burner designed by Sir James Douglass. Its initial intensity was 2,000 candlepower as compared with 1,700 for the eight wick burner at the Bishop. When magnified by the huge lens of the optical apparatus however the power of the Round Island light was less than that of the Bishop as it had to pass through red glass because the station character at that time was a red flash. When it was replaced in 1967 the task of rescuing it for posterity was deemed too difficult and it was broken up on site.

The replacement optic was a flat panel, mounted on a gearless pedestal, and carrying a bank of 20 sealed beam units (car headlamps). It looked quite insignificant in the huge lantern built to accommodate the original optic. This panel has now become a museum piece itself as a result of the automation work and hopefully will be preserved. It has been replaced with a small rotating optic with a 1,000 watt metal halide lamp as the light source, powered by solar power from 2003.

STATION CHARACTERISTICS

Light: one white flash every ten seconds, intensity 340,000 candela, range 24 miles.
Fog signal: Nautophone giving four blasts every 60 seconds.

Round Island lighthouse. AUTHOR'S COLLECTION

Peninnis Head lighthouse. AUTHOR'S COLLECTION

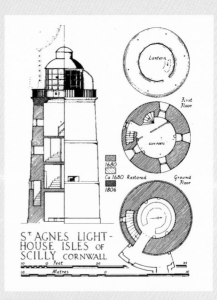

St Agnes Light-
House Isles of
Scilly Cornwall

COURTESY: DOUGLAS HAGUE

PENINNIS HEAD LIGHTHOUSE
[SV 912093]
This lighthouse is built on the southern extremity of St Mary's island in the Isles of Scilly and leads shipping safely into St Mary's Sound. It is a steel trestle tower with the upper part plated to form a service room below the lantern and the height from the ground to gallery is 30 feet.

The light is automatic, the lens revolving around the light source. Until recently it had to be checked and the weight that drove the light wound up daily. It was originally lit by oil gas when erected in 1911 and was converted to operate on compressed acetylene gas in 1920. This is supplied in large. cylinders brought over from the mainland when needed, about twice a year The remains of the concrete supports for the old oil gas tanks can still be seen in the compound surrounding the station. After the light was brought into service in 1911 the old St Agnes light was discontinued. The lighthouse is not open to visitors.
STATION CHARACTERISTICS:
Light: one white flash every 20 seconds, intensity 4,500 candela, range 17 miles.
Fog signal: none.

ST AGNES LIGHTHOUSE
[SV 881083]
Although no longer in use no lighthouse more richly deserves a place in our story of Lighthouse Heritage than this one. Situated on the tiny island of the same name in the Isles of Scilly it has stood guard for the mariner since 1680. It was almost the first lighthouse ever erected by Trinity House and it continued to show a warning light until 1911.

St Agnes, Isles of Scilly. S J NEWBURY, RNAS CULDROSE

The light was from a coal fire for the first one hundred and ten years after which it was converted to oil lamps in 1790. This followed the invention of the circular wick by Ami Argand in 1782. There were 21 of these lamps, each with its own reflector, and they were mounted on a triangular frame with seven on each side. The apparatus was made to revolve by means of a descending weight and regulated to make one revolution every minute giving three separate bright flashes in that period.

The coal fire was burned in a large cresset or fire basket and the one in use at the time of conversion to an oil light is still preserved as a museum piece on the island of Tresco. No doubt this grate is the last of several that must have burnt out previously since we know that the average consumption of coal for this lighthouse was 107 tons a year. It was delivered by ship once a year and provided a welcome opportunity for local labour to earn some extra money.

In 1911 a decision was made to erect a new light on Peninnis Head on the island of St May's and as a result the St Agnes light was discontinued. The tower is now a private dwelling but is still painted white and provides a useful daymark for seafarers in the vicinity.

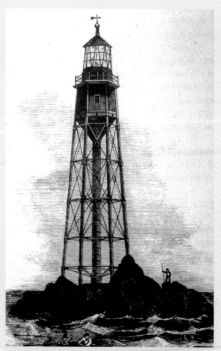

The first tower at Bishop Rock built 1847–50 and destroyed before occupation.
TRINITY HOUSE COLLECTION

BISHOP ROCK LIGHTHOUSE
[SV 807065]

Built on an isolated rock only just large enough to accommodate it this famous lighthouse is subject to the full force of the Atlantic storms which have claimed so many wrecks in the Isles of Scilly. The most famous of these was *HMS Association* which was lost quite close to the Bishop taking her Admiral, Sir Cloudesley Shovel and 1,800 men from his fleet to their deaths in 1703. But it was another century and a half before Trinity House finally succeeded in establishing a lighthouse here on what is acknowledged to be one of the most difficult sites in the world.

The first tower erected here was an open structure carried on six cast iron columns sunk into the rock. It was designed like this to let the sea pass freely between them with the least amount of resistance. It took three years to erect and was ready to receive the lighting apparatus when it was totally destroyed by a violent storm on 5 February 1850. Fortunately without any loss of life.

Work commenced on a replacement tower in stone the following year and this was completed in 1858. The rough granite for this was obtained from Carnsew and Lamorna quarries on the mainland and the blocks were dressed to the required shapes in a workyard on St Mary's Island. They were then carried to the rock in barges and landed by manual labour.

After its completion it was soon realised that this tower was not strong enough to resist the immense weight of water which crashed against it in bad weather. It vibrated very considerably, objects were shaken from tables and shelves and some of the prisms in the lantern were fractured. Later on some of the granite blocks were split and the tower had to be strengthened from top to bottom with heavy iron rods.

Even this remedial work was not sufficient and in 1881 Trinity House

The second tower at Bishop Rock, here being strengthened and heightened in the 1880s
GIBSON COLLECTION

Bishop Rock. AUTHOR'S COLLECTION

decided to strengthen the tower again and to increase its height. This was done by giving the whole lighthouse an outer casing of masonry from its foundation up to the service room just below the lantern and then adding a further three rooms above that one. All the new outside blocks were dovetailed horizontally and vertically to each other and each stone up to course eight had a male dovetail, six inches in depth on the inside face to ensure it had a perfect connection with the tower.

In addition the blocks up to and including the twentieth course were each secured by two Muntz metal bolts, $^1/_2$ inch diameter, passing through them and into the block below. During all of the considerable amount of work involved a temporary light was maintained from the tower which was raised on a stout pole as the extra floors were built underneath it. This work was accomplished without any loss of life despite very difficult conditions in less than $3^1/_2$ years.

Undoubtedly the speed at which this was done was due in very great measure to the steam power provided by the Trinity

House ship *Hercules* She was transferred to this work immediately after completing the fifth Eddystone tower in 1882. Three sets of moorings were laid down for her use, fairly close to the tower and she moored between them and the tower with large coir ropes 13 inches in circumference. Coir is a springy waterproof rope made from coconut fibre. With a moderate ground sea the movement of the ship was sometimes so great that even these large ropes parted one after another. The weight of the extra stone added at this time amounted to 3,220 tons, making a total of 5,720. On completion of this work a new lantern was fitted and a new optical apparatus inside. This is still in use and consists of two sets of lenses one above the other with a total height of 15 feet. The light source for each was an eight wick oil burner. In clear weather only one of these was in use but when the visibility was reduced so that the light at St Agnes was not seen then both lamps were lit.

The light source was subsequently altered to an oil vapour lamp using a mantle and in 1973 it was altered again when electricity was installed. This was soon followed by the installation of a helideck above the lantern in 1976. The top set of lenses were removed for preservation. Since December 1992 the station has been un-manned.

STATION CHARACTERISTICS:

Light: two white flashes every 15 seconds, intensity 600,000 candela, range 24 miles.
Fog signal: electric, giving two blasts every 90 seconds, one long and one short.

TATER DU LIGHTHOUSE
[SW 440231]
This latest addition to the impressive list of Cornish lighthouses was built on a headland of the same name on the south coast of the Lands End peninsular as recently as 1965. The need for it is clearly documented in any book about Cornish shipwrecks and the surprise is that the date of construction is not 1865 instead.

The final spur that was needed to persuade Trinity House to erect it was the tragic wreck of the Spanish coaster *Juan Ferrer*. She ran ashore on Boscawen point, half a mile west of Tater Du with the loss of 11 lives on 23 October 1963 and this prompted a number of petitions for this section of the coast to be marked with a light.

It was decided that a small light for purely local needs would give insufficient warning and it was considered necessary to provide a light and fog signal powerful enough to aid general navigation as well. The tower was designed by Trinity House, built by Messrs Humphreys Ltd of Knightsbridge and was fully automatic and un-manned from its beginning. The opening ceremony was performed on 7 July 1965 by HRH The Duke of Gloucester who was then Master of Trinity House.

The navigation light is from an electric filament lamp in a revolving optic and is operated from batteries which are float-charged from the mains grid supply. The batteries alone will operate the light for five days and a stand-by diesel driven generator will charge them in the event of a prolonged mains failure. The light is switched on and off by time switch and the optic is fitted with four separate lamps in a lamp changer. This will automatically bring one of the spare lamps into focus if there is a failure of one in use. A separate lamp is installed 10 feet lower down the

Tater Du lighthouse. AUTHOR'S COLLECTION

tower which shows a fixed red light over the Runnelstone rock to the west of the station.

The fog signal was provided by a stack of powerful electric emitters, but the 72 loud speaker units that were built into the tower itself have now been removed.

STATION CHARACTERISTICS:

Main light: three white flashes every 15 seconds, intensity 294,000 candela, range 23 miles.

Subsidiary light: showing fixed red over an arc of 17 degrees covering the Runnelstone rock.

Fog signal: two blasts every 30 seconds.

LIZARD LIGHTHOUSE
[SW 700100]

This is the oldest mainland lighthouse in Cornwall and is world famous for its powerful light which has a range of 29 miles. It began as a private light first established in 1619 by Sir John Killigrew against fierce opposition from two different sources. This came from the local inhabitants who foresaw a decrease in the wrecks which were a frequent occurrence

Lizard eastern tower in 1812 after the coal fire was replaced by Argand lamps.
TRINITY HOUSE COLLECTION

Lizard lighthouse with eastern and western lanterns. AUTHOR'S COLLECTION

and provided rich pickings for them, and secondly from Trinity House itself. This was early in its history when the Elder Brethren were reluctant to undertake the work of lighthouse building themselves and disliked the idea of one being outside their control if it was built privately. This light was not a success and was abandoned in 1623 as ship owners were unwilling to pay any light dues for its upkeep and nothing more was done until 1752.

In that year two towers were erected under a patent granted to Trinity House but then leased by them to Thomas Fonnerau for 61 years at an annual rent of £80. Both the towers carried a coal fire and there was a cottage between them from which a man known as an overlooker could see the fires and check that the stokers were maintaining a good light. If not he would rouse them by a blast from a cowhorn.

Those two towers are the ones still standing today, a little altered but substantially the same with 6 dwellings for lighthouse keepers between them. In 1812 the coal fires were discontinued in favour of Argand oil lights with reflectors which remained in use until 1878 when electric light was installed using generators at the lighthouse. At the same time a foghorn was installed. Trinity House had been experimenting with electricity to light their lighthouse for some years prior to this, principally at the South Foreland station in Kent. When they introduced this at the

Lizard lighthouse. Gordon Hill

Lizard one generator was installed and a second was added in 1881. This had been on show at the Paris Exhibition and is still in existence at the lighthouse today.

The two electric lights were still fixed ones, i.e. not flashing ones, until 1903. Then the light in the Western tower was discontinued and a single flashing one installed in the Eastern tower. This was an arc lamp which rotated and it produced 12 million candle power. It is said that several bad pilchard seasons which followed this were blamed on the power of this light and a petition was sent to Trinity House to have it reduced. What effect this petition had is not known but in 1926 the light was replaced with a three kilowatt electric filament lamp producing four million candle power

Briefly the Lizard became a control station for the automatic off-shore stations in the Lands End area but all stations are now monitored from Harwich. The original engine room is retained in working condition, although not used as an aid to navigation, and with the tower is open to the public as a visitor centre.

Station characteristics:
Light: one white flash every three seconds, intensity 8000,000 candela, range 26 miles.
Fog signal: electric, giving two blasts every 60 seconds.

ST ANTHONY'S HEAD LIGHTHOUSE
[SW 846312]

This lighthouse dates from 1835 and was erected during the great Victorian era of lighthouse building. It marks the entrance to Falmouth Harbour and stands on the eastern side just above high water level where it helps to guide shipping clear of the Black Rock in the centre of the channel.

It is also intended to warn vessels away

St Anthony Head lighthouse and Falmouth harbour, 1880s. Trinity House collection

St Anthony Head lighthouse. AUTHOR'S COLLECTION

light was provided by a pressure vapour burner and was again altered in 1954 when mains electricity was connected to the station and the light is now an electric flashing one. There is a stand-by generator which starts automatically in the event of a mains failure.

The lighthouse was not equipped with a fog signal at first but subsequently it was given a huge bell weighing two tons and said to be larger than any bell in Cornwall. This bell was removed in 1954 when an electric fog signal was installed together with a fog detector to bring it into action. The bell was then sent to Penwerris church on permanent loan but it proved too expensive to have it installed. The bell was eventually sent to a foundry at Loughborough to be melted down.

When the light was first exhibited 20 April 1835 was Easter Monday and a fine day. This attracted a huge crowd to witness the commissioning ceremony and the scene resembled a fair with a great number of booths erected. Today the station is fully automated.

STATION CHARACTERISTICS:

Light: white isophase 15 seconds with a red sector over the Manacles rocks, range 22 miles (white), 20 miles (red).

Fog signal: one blast every 30 seconds.

EDDYSTONE LIGHTHOUSE

Erected to mark the very dangerous Eddystone rocks lying eight miles 192 degrees from Rame Head [SX 418481] and although not generally considered as a Cornish lighthouse it certainly lies off the Cornish coast and not the Devon one. The present tower is built of Cornish granite from Delank quarry and is the last of five which have marked this danger since 1698. The first tower was built by Henry Winstanley and completed in that year. This was the very first lighthouse ever built on a wave swept rock which was totally surrounded by deep water. It had to be strengthened after the first winter and was virtually re-built in fact, but it then survived for another four years. During that time it saved countless lives and many ships from destruction and proved to the world that such exposed and difficult dangers could indeed be mastered. It was destroyed on the night of 26 November 1703 during a most violent storm.

from the dangerous Manacles rocks off Porthoustock to the south and with its range of 22 miles the light serves as a 'passing light' to shipping in the Channel beyond the Lizard point. By taking cross bearings of this light and the Lizard light a prudent watch-keeper could track his course very accurately and calculate the set of the tide. Nowadays the introduction of electronic aids has largely superseded the need for such checks.

Work on building the lighthouse began in May 1834, the builder being Olver of Falmouth, and the light was first exhibited on 20 April 1835. The designer was James Walker, Trinity House engineer and the octagonal tower had living quarters for two keepers with provision for a temporary relief keeper for periods of leave or sickness.

When first opened the light was shown from eight Argand oil lamps revolving by means of a weight descending in a tube in the centre of the tower. Subsequently the

Unfortunately Winstanley himself was on board and perished with his masterpiece.

The third tower was built by John Rudyerd, using ship building principles, and was completed in 1708. He made it narrow and tapering to offer the least resistance possible to the sea, ballasted with many tons of stone to give it stability, built with a ship's mast up through its centre for flexibility and then sheathed with heavy planks caulked with oakum and pitch to make it watertight. He also dispensed with all the useless decoration which was such an extraordinary feature of the earlier one, thus giving it the smoothest possible exterior. This tower stood for 47 years and was then burnt down when the candles in the lantern set fire to the roof.

The three keepers were rescued next morning having been badly burned by the mixture of blazing wood and molten lead from the roof covering which fell on them throughout the night. One man was hit in the face by hot lead and some of it passed down his throat. After his rescue no one believed this story, thinking that the poor man was demented. He survived for 12 days and then died. His doctor carried out an autopsy on his body and removed a piece of lead weighing over seven ounces from the pit of his stomach. This gruesome relic is still on exhibition in the Royal Scottish museum in Edinburgh.

The fourth tower was designed and built by John Smeaton between 1756 and 1759 using completely new principles. He decided to build his tower almost entirely of stone blocks and to cut dovetails in them to hold the whole lot in one solid mass. This was the first occasion that such a revolutionary idea had been used but it has since been copied by lighthouse builders all over the world. Like its predecessors this tower also used candles for its warning light, but in 1810 these were replaced by Argand lamps which burnt oil using hollow cylindrical wicks and a glass chimney.

Smeatons tower stood for 127 years

Winstanley's Eddystone Lighthouse, 1699.

Rudyerd's Eddystone Lighthouse, 1709.

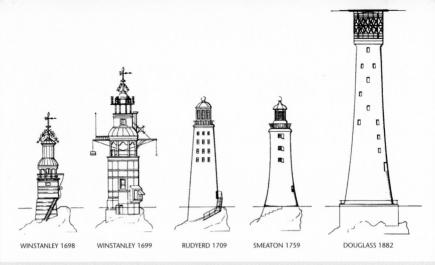

WINSTANLEY 1698   WINSTANLEY 1699   RUDYERD 1709   SMEATON 1759   DOUGLASS 1882

The five lighthouses built on the Eddystone Rock since 1698. TRINITY HOUSE COLLECTION

until the rock on which it was built began to show signs of cracking and a replacement was ordered. When that one was finished a public subscription was raised by the people of Plymouth to pay for Smeatons tower to be taken down as far as the solid base and re-erected on Plymouth Hoe where it still stands more than a hundred years on. It was commemorated after 100 years on the reef by the engraving of a tiny lighthouse at the feet of Britannia on the back of the old penny then in use.

The fifth tower is the one now standing, much taller and heavier than any of the earlier ones. It was designed by James Douglass who was afterwards knighted by Queen Victoria for his work. He also designed a special ship, the *Hercules*, to carry the three ton stone blocks and she was able to use her own steam winch to hoist them into place. All the previous towers had been built entirely by hand. It was completed in 1882 and after a century of use it looks fit to last another hundred years with ease.

This tower has seen several major improvements in lighthouse technology during its life.

The light was altered from oil burning to electric power in 1956. The fog signal was altered from a bell to an explosive sound and then to an electronic sound emitter. A helideck was fitted above the lantern in 1980 and the station was converted to automatic operation and unmanned in 1982.

STATION CHARACTERISTICS:
Main light: two white flashes every 10 seconds, intensity 199,000 candela, range 22 miles.
Subsidiary light: fixed red from a separate window halfway down the tower over an arc of 17 degrees. This is to mark the Hand Deep, a dangerous shoal 3½ miles NW of the station.
Fog signal: electric, giving three blasts every 60 seconds.

Eddystone late 1881. Douglass's lighthouse nearing completion with Smeaton's lighthouse behind. AUTHOR'S COLLECTION

SECONDARY LIGHTS

Any book about Cornwall's famous lights must also include details of the 'second team' which are known as Secondary Lights; those lesser powered but no less important ones which mark our harbours, docks and river mouths and lead the mariner to his final destination. This was another benefit bequeathed to us by those energetic Victorian engineers who contrived to mark every one of the ports and harbours around our coast before the end of their century.

Apart from the lighthouse on St Anthony Head at the entrance to Falmouth all these harbour 'lead in' lights are un-manned and are of fairly routine construction. Many of them are simple fixed lights i.e. not flashing, mounted on a wall or a pole but five of them are miniature lighthouses, at Newlyn, Penzance, Fowey and two at St Ives.

PADSTOW HARBOUR
[SW920755]
A conspicuous stone daymark on Stepper Point marks the entrance to the River Camel and nearby there is a white light flashing every ten seconds visible four miles. St Saviours Point carries a green light flashing every ten seconds and the harbour entrance is marked by two fixed green lights, vertical, on the north side and two red ones, vertical, on the south.

NEWQUAY HARBOUR
[SW807620]
The North pier head has two fixed green vertical lights and the south pier two fixed red vertical ones, all visible two miles.

HAYLE HARBOUR
[SW550380]
The west side of the channel has a man made training bank marked by a line of perches (pole beacons). Called a training bank because it trains the strong out going ebb tide to keep to the same line and so scour a channel across the sand bar at the harbour entrance. There are two fixed white leading lights on pile structures, visible four miles, which, if kept in line, lead vessels into the harbour entrance.

The old secondary light on Smeaton's Pier, St Ives.
ALAN KITTRIDGE

ST IVES
[SW321406]
The oldest secondary light is halfway along Smeaton's Pier, erected about 1831. This is a squat four-sided stone tower with an eight sided gallery holding the gas-lit lantern and has been disused since this pier was extended in 1890. It burnt out due to arson in 1996 but was restored with a new dome and lantern. The pier end is now marked by a white cast iron eight sided tower which carries two fixed red lights vertically disposed, visible three miles. There are two fixed green ones also vertical on the end of the east pier, visible five miles.

ST MARY'S HARBOUR
[SV902110]
There is a fixed green light visible three miles on the outer end of the pier

MOUSEHOLE HARBOUR
[SW470264]
Two fixed green lights vertical, visible four miles. These are replaced by a fixed red light when the harbour is closed.

NEWLYN
[SW4682871
Round, white, cast iron tower with red base and cupola on the south pier end. The light is a white flash every five seconds, visible ten miles, over an arc of 83 degrees to the south-east. On the north pier end is a fixed green/white light visible two miles. The white is visible over the harbour and the green sector shows over an arc of ten degrees to the north east. There is a fixed red light, visible one mile on the end of the old quay.

47

Penzance harbour light. ALAN KITTRIDGE

PENZANCE
[SW479302]
Round, white, cast iron tower with red base and cupola on the south pier end.The light is a white flash every five seconds, visible ten miles, over an arc of 83 degrees to the south-east. The fog horn has been discontinued. On the north pier end is a fixed green/white light visible two miles. The white is visible over the harbour and the green sector shows over an arc often degrees to the north east.There is a fixed red light, visible one mile on the end of the old quay

PORTHLEVEN HARBOUR
[SW627256]
Fixed green light on South Pier Head visible four miles.

FALMOUTH HARBOUR
[SW830330]
In addition to St Anthony Head lighthouse recorded elsewhere there is a red light flashing every two seconds, visible three miles on the Eastern Breakwater, a quick flashing white light visible three miles on the end of the North Arm and two fixed red vertical lights on St Mawes quay head.

MEVAGISSEY HARBOUR
[SX 018448]
South Pier head has a white light showing two flashes every ten seconds visible 12 miles. Foghorn giving one blast every 30 seconds.

CHARLESTOWN
[SX 0395i6]
A fixed green light on the North Breakwater and a fixed red on the South one. In addition harbour signals from a flag staff indicate 'harbour closed' – red light (night) or black shape (day) 'harbour open' – green light (night) or red ensign (day).

PAR
[SX 079528]
There are no pier head 'lead in' lights in this harbour only entry signals. These consist of a red shape by day or a red light at night to signify that the port is closed or a vessel is leaving.

FOWEY HARBOUR
[SX 125515]
The lighthouse on St Catherine's Point at the harbour entrance is a white octagonal tower with a red lantern. It carries a light giving one flash every five seconds which shows white in the centre of the channel and red on each side of it. Inside the harbour is a leading light on Whitehouse Point shown from a very large lantern on a pole. It leads ships up the centre of the harbour by showing an isophase light every three seconds in three colours. The centre one is white over a ten degree arc, to the west is a red arc and to the east is a green one, both of five degrees. The north pier head on Whitehouse Point carries two fixed red lights vertical, on a red post, visible eight miles.

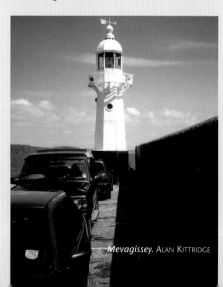

Mevagissey. ALAN KITTRIDGE

Whitehouse Point, Fowey. ALAN KITTRIDGE

POLPERRO HARBOUR
[SX 213508]
A quick flashing white light on Spy House Point visible eight miles has a red sector to the east and another to the west. In the tidal basin a fixed white light visible four miles is shown from the west pier and is changed to red if the harbour is closed in bad weather

LOOE HARBOUR
[SX 258530]
On the pier head is a white occulting light every three seconds which has a red sector to the north east and another smaller one to the south east. The white light is visible IS miles and the red ones 12 miles. A fog horn on Nailzee Point gives two blasts every 30 seconds.

BEACONS OR DAYMARKS

In addition to these secondary lights there are a number of unlighted beacons, some of which are described elsewhere in the book as well.

PORTREATH
[SW 656457]
A white conical tower 25 feet high on the east side of the harbour 123 feet above high water. Erected to assist sailing ships to identify the entrance. It originally had a weather vane and tide signals were shown when the harbour was used commercially.

ST MARTIN'S DAYMARK, ISLES OF SCILLY
[SV 942162]
This was erected in 1687 and is about 40 feet high. Put up to distinguish the Northern limit of the islands following the erection of the St Agnes lighthouse in 1680. It is a hollow round tower surmounted by a cone and painted in red and white horizontal bands. There is a flight of steps inside but the entrance is now sealed.

CROW ROCK
[SV9 10132]
A pole painted in black and red horizontal bands and carrying two black balls to indicate an isolated rock.

WOOLPACK
[SV 898098]
This beacon marks the outer extremity, under water, of the Woolpack Point in St Mary's Sound. It is a pole painted yellow above black and carries two black cones point down to indicate safe water to the south.

RUNNELSTONE
[SW 369217]
Two beacons in line which indicate the rock of that name one mile to seaward. North one black conical, south one red pyramid.

GEAR
[SW 480294]
A pole painted black and red horizontal bands and carrying a radar reflector plus two black balls to indicate an isolated rock.

Runnelstone beacon, Gwennap Head. ALAN KITTRIDGE

49

CRESSAR
[SW 485305]
A pole painted yellow above black and carrying a radar reflector plus two black cones point down to indicate safe water to the south of it.

RYMAN or RAYMOND
[SW 496305]
Exactly the same as the Cressar

VROGUE
Two pairs of beacons, one on Beast Head [5W716118] erected in 1859 and one on The Balk [SW715129] erected 1860. When these pairs are in line, seen from seaward, they both lead over the Vrogue rock approximately half a mile out, thus indicating the greatest danger. The Beast or Bass pair are red and white vertical lines on the side of the old signal station and also on a short wall lower down the cliff, beside the coastal path. The Balk pair consist of a large white diamond shape mounted on a wooden frame which is painted in red and white bands on the cliff top and a white painted mark on an off-lying rock known as the Middle Hummock (Warning — it is not visible from the cliff edge).

BLACK ROCK, FALMOUTH
[SW 834318]
A pole painted in black and red horizontal bands and carrying two black balls to indicate an isolated rock.

GRIBBEN HEAD
[SX 098498]
A stone tower 84 feet high painted in red and white bands. Erected in 1832 to assist sailing ships to identify the headland and St Austell Bay while far out to sea. It was requisitioned by the Admiralty during the last war to serve as a lookout station. There is a flight of steps inside but the tower is not open to the public.

BUOYS
There are no off shore sand banks around Cornwall to require a multitude of buoys as there are on the east coast of England. Consequently there are only a few buoys which mark isolated rocks. The Runnelstone and Stones buoys are 1st class (the biggest) and weigh ten tons. The others are 2nd class and weigh nearly six tons. All are moored by a chain with links $1^{1}/_{2}$ inches in diameter and either a five ton or a three ton sinker on the end. The principal ones are all lighted and their details are as follows:

STONES BUOY, ST IVES BAY
[SW 562447]
This buoy marks the outer end of the reef which extends $1^{1}/_{2}$ miles from Godrevy lighthouse. It is painted black above yellow and carries two black cones point up. It shows a quick flashing white light and carries a whistle and a bell.

RUNNELSTONE BUOY
[SW 370200]
Laid on the south side of the rock and painted yellow above black and carrying two black cones point down. It shows a white light giving six quick flashes plus one long flash every 15 seconds, and carries a bell and a whistle.

LOW LEE BUOY
[SW 48l278]
Laid on the east side of the rock and painted black, yellow, black horizontally and carrying two cones base to base. It shows a white light giving three flashes every ten seconds.

MANACLES BUOY
[SW822206]
This is identical to the Low Lee buoy.

Balk beacon, The Lizard. ALAN KITTRIDGE